The Bronx Bombers

A CELEBRATION OF THE 1985 NEW YORK YANKEES

UNITED PRESS INTERNATIONAL

CONTEMPORARY
BOOKS, INC.
CHICAGO

CONTENTS

1

A SHORT SEASON FOR YOGI

Yogi Berra was the manager of the 1985 New York Yankees, and he was rolling along just fine . . . until they played the national anthem in Fenway Park on Opening Day.

It seemed unfair. The Yankees were still fresh and tan from spring training, and already the rumors of a firing had begun. From coast to coast, even people familiar with George Steinbrenner's whims were shocked.

Ah yes, George Steinbrenner, owner of ships and the New York Yankees. The man who had brought pennant and World Series excitement to New York had also brought an atmosphere of eccentricity, zaniness, and turbulence.

While most baseball owners prefer their presence to be distant, passive, and aloof, Steinbrenner is just the opposite. Since buying the team, he has changed managers 11 times. He has made it clear that he is entitled to do it again and whenever he wishes, like after two straight defeats or an ill-fated pitching decision. Owners can do such things.

Baseball scribes had predicted the 1985 season would be a sedate one. From spring training camp they filed bulletins suggesting Steinbrenner had matured. He understood what can happen over a long season. He decreed as late as spring training that Berra's job was safe through the end of the season. Sixteen games into the season, he changed his mind .

So much for a sedate season. Billy Martin, the Bad Brilliant Yankee, returned for his fourth tour at the helm.

The two moves were vigorously denounced in the press. What had happened to honor? To hallowed traditions? What was Steinbrenner thinking? Why would he break his word? Wasn't this surely a portent of a disastrous season? And you could bet Martin would soon anger his boss and be gone by July.

YANKEE AXIOMS

In pinstripes, all things are possible. These early-season changes simply meant the Yankees were just being the Yankees.

A short season it was—16 games to be exact, when Steinbrenner decided to make a managerial change.

Remember, if you are a Yankee, life must not be boring. You need a little drama, controversy, turmoil, a shakeup or two, a firing or three. Besides, George Steinbrenner, a man who honors pinstripes above all things, had to remain faithful to Yankee axioms. One of those axioms begins with the following premise: the Yankees don't really play in the American League. The Yankees play in New York City and New York's first allegiance is to winners.

By mid-August Yogi was the dim past, Billy Martin IV was a genius (again), the Yankees were winning, and the fans were cheering—40,000 of them a game. Time heals all wounds, if you end up in first place. That's another Yankee axiom.

In April it seemed that Berra's low-key personality would be perfect for the Yan-

Yogi just can't seem to get the breaks.

kees' latest compilation of high-priced, high-strung talent. The Yankees had the look of a contender in the spring, the biggest question being their pitching. Phil Niekro was aging, Ron Guidry was coming off a bad year, and they represented the core of the staff. Right-hander Joe Cowley threw hard, but had a reputation as a practical joker. It was said he would only produce when he knew he had your attention. Left-hander Dennis Rasmussen was young and questionable. Ed Whitson had been signed from the San Diego Padres as a free agent and you never know about them.

If the pitching proved effective, the Yankees could provide some offense. Outfielder Dave Winfield was considered one of the best players in the league, and first baseman Don Mattingly had won the American League batting title the previous season. In addition, the Yankees had gone to great trouble for the right to make outfielder Rickey Henderson a rich man. He would provide speed at the top of the lineup and play a vigorous center field.

Were there other potential problems? Of course. Second baseman Willie Randolph had lost a step and the third base platoon of Dale Berra and Mike Pagliarulo looked particularly suspect.

Entering the 1985 season, Steinbrenner was especially anxious that the team play well. One year before, the Detroit Tigers had sprinted to a huge early lead and wound up winning the World Series. That was after Steinbrenner sarcastically declared in spring training that "Yogi assures me everything will be fine."

Well, it wasn't fine. If the Yankees started poorly once again, no matter what decrees he had made, Steinbrenner would be of little disposition to be patient.

EARLY RUMBLINGS

The Yankees lost 9–2 on Opening Day. Boston pitcher Dennis "Oil Can" Boyd frustrated Dave Winfield with both his theatrics and his pitching. The Yankees lost the second game of the season 14–5. Ed Whitson got shelled. Rumblings began. If there was ever a time to panic, it was then. With *only* 160 games left to play, Steinbrenner announced the third game was "crucial" to Yankee chances.

The season was all of two days old and already the Yankees were two games back. It didn't get better. The Yankees lost the "crucial" third game 6–4.

On April 13, the Yankees beat Cleveland 6–3, triggering a four-game winning streak. Sixteen games into the season, though, they were 6–10. Rumblings continued. The "impossible" was rumored to be happening. Berra was going and Martin was returning.

During the final game of a three-game series against Chicago, in which the Yankees were losing, the decision was made.

After the game, players found a press release waiting in their lockers.

Don Baylor sailed a trashcan across the room, spewing garbage all over the clubhouse. Don Mattingly restrained himself until safely inside the trainer's room, from which reporters are barred. The sounds he made as he hurled objects throughout the room were difficult to translate into quotes, but it was expressive. Only Henderson, who had played under Billy in Oakland, voiced pleasure over the return of Martin, and as he spoke to the press, teammates glared.

Berra finally emerged from his office, and made his final rounds in the locker room, shaking hands and embracing players.

"I have no regrets," said Berra. "I don't think my players laid down on me and tried to lose. I still think this club will come around. He's the boss, and I'm used to it."

Berra had been fired by the Yankees as manager in 1964 and as Met manager in '75.

"That's the way this game is. My contract doesn't say I have to do anything if I'm fired, so I'm going to go home and play golf."

Billy was back and good ol' #1 was looking for another pennant.

MARTIN: BEST AGAINST THE ODDS

Martin inherited a 6–10 team struggling in nearly every aspect of the game. Yet, while he was not guaranteed the position to manage the rest of the year, one thing seemed designed for Martin: he was at his best as an underdog.

His trademark, as a manager, had been

Billy cracked a smile when he returned for his fourth tour at the helm.

the ability to inherit a dispirited team, then show it how to win by throwing strikes and hitting the cutoff man. Billy Martin teams will bunt and take the extra base. They will out-hustle the other team.

Martin managed Minnesota for one year (1969) and produced a West Division title. In Detroit, he took an aging fourth-place squad and finished second in 1971 and first in the East in 1972. In 1974, he brought the Texas Rangers into second place, a considerable improvement over their sixth-place stature the previous year. Finally, in Oakland, he took the A's from seventh place to second in 1980 then first in 1981. The man can manage.

And, there is no doubt he lives to manage the Yankees. After guiding the team to a pennant in 1976 and a World Series championship in '77, he was fired midway

New York's first allegiance is to winning, and Billy knows that Winfield must produce for the Yanks to stay on top.

Billy always makes himself accessible to his players. Here he congratulates Mike Pagliarulo after the Yanks downed the Royals.

Billy only wishes Mickey would suit-up for the 1985 season.

The reconstruction begins. Here Billy gives
personal instruction to catcher Butch Wynegar.

Billy always chooses his friends carefully.

through the 1978 season when Bob Lemon took over. In the middle of the 1979 season, Lemon was out and Billy was back in. But that winter he was involved in an altercation with a marshmallow salesman in a Bloomington, Minnesota, bar—it spelled the end of his second reign.

In 1980, Dick Howser was given the job and the team won 103 regular-season games, but lost to Kansas City in the American League playoffs. Howser did not return. In '81, Gene Michael made it to September before Steinbrenner brought back Lemon to finish the season. 1982 was a record year, in which Lemon, Michael, and General Manager Clyde King all made pit stops in the manager's office.

In '83, Martin made his third tour of duty under a five-year contract and the team finished third. But it was not a good year for Billy. His behavior was erratic. He sometimes showed up late to the ballpark, and often holed up in his office behind a closed door. Once, in Cleveland, he slept in the shower room while his amazed players watched.

Berra was hired in 1984, and somehow kept the job the entire season. The Yankees recorded the best post-All-Star Game record in baseball in a futile attempt to catch the runaway Tigers. But Detroit outclassed everyone, including the Padres in the World Series.

Martin was already in Texas scouting the Rangers when the end came for Berra, and he waited there for the Yankees to join him.

"Yogi was their friend," he said before his first game back on the bench. "And I'm Yogi's friend, too. But he left not because of his friendship with them, but because they put him in last place. I'm not here to win a popularity contest. I'm here to win ball games. I don't care if a couple of players hate me. All I care about is if they produce."

Billy Martin, a manager made of contradictions, began his fourth coming on a Monday night in Texas. And the Yankees lost 7–5.

Billy Ball has many characteristics. Here Dale Berra demonstrates the most important ingredient, hustle, as he breaks up a double play.

2

THE YANKEE THEORY OF WINNING

Broadcaster Red Barber used to call Yankee Stadium the "big ballpark" because of its size and tradition. Since opening in 1923, it has been recognized as an eccentric ballpark.

Yankee Stadium has always favored left-handed power hitters and left-handed pitchers. In right field, left-handed hitters were able to shoot for a "porch" that was only 344 feet away. In left field, however, even titanic drives would die and be caught in "Death Valley," which was 457 feet from home plate.

The theory of winning at Yankee Stadium was simple. Your lineup must contain left-handed hitters with a good power stroke. You must assemble good defense and competent pitching in the hope of keeping the game close. Then, you waited for someone to hit a three-run homer into the "porch" in the seventh or eighth inning. Someone usually did.

The Yankee tradition of pennants and World Series championships coincided with the arrival of Babe Ruth from Boston, which, in turn, nearly coincided with the building of Yankee Stadium.

You've heard the moniker, "The House That Ruth Built." In 1923, the Yankees used the formula to win the pennant by 16 games. Ruth hit 41 homers and left-hander Herb Pennock posted a 19–6 record.

The formula rarely varied over the years. In 1927, Ruth hit 60 homers and Lou Gehrig, 47. Pennock went 19–8 and Dutch Ruether 13–6. In the pennant years of 1936, '37, '38, and '39, the Yankees offered a variety of left-handed sluggers who, at various times, included Gehrig, Bill Dickey, Red Rolfe, George Selkirk, and Tommy Henrich, while Lefty Gomez was the principal contributor to the pitching staff.

When the Yankees won their record five World Series titles in 1949–53, lefty Eddie Lopat was never less than five games over .500 in a season. He also had help from Whitey Ford and Johnny Sain. Meanwhile, Tommy Henrich, Yogi Berra, and Mickey Mantle kept hitting the ball over the fence.

In the years 1960–64, Mantle and Roger Maris provided power, while Ford anchored the staff.

Left-handed hitting and left-handed pitching could be an oversimplification—an oversimplification that won an awful lot of pennants.

When the Yankees returned to glory in 1976, their victories carried a familiar look, even though Yankee Stadium had been modified with a longer distance to right field and a shorter shot to left. Roy White, Graig Nettles, Chris Chambliss, and Oscar Gamble hit the ball out of the park. Sparky Lyle came out of the bullpen to save 23 games. The following year, the Yankees added Reggie Jackson's 32 homers and the left-handed arms of Ron Guidry and Don Gullett.

By 1985, the Yankees did not look especially like the traditional Yankee Stadium club. Of their left-handers, Guidry was coming off a 10–11 year. Dennis Rasmussen had appeared in only 28 major-league games. Dave Righetti had pitched well in short relief, but the concern was that the Yankee pitching staff could not deliver him a lead in the late innings.

'85 FORMULA

The '85 Yankee lineup does not follow the Yankee lineups of the past. Dave Winfield and Don Baylor were right-handed and despite shorter distances to left and "Death Valley" in left center, you still needed a good poke to get it out of the park. Don Mattingly was a lefty and had 23 homers the previous year, and he's more of a line-drive hitter rather than a power man.

The biggest question was Rickey Henderson. Here was someone who stole lots of bases, but the Yankee game was the three-run homer, not baseball one base at a time.

Nevertheless, the formula proved successful. Guidry bounced back with Cy Young Award credentials. Mattingly proved he could hit for power, both at

Joe DiMaggio tips his cap to a standing ovation.

Even after the left field fences were brought in 19 feet, the alleys in Yankee Stadium remain some of
the longest in baseball.

Bobby Brown, President of the American
League, and Joe DiMaggio smile upon their
return to Yankee Stadium.

Yankee Stadium and on the road. Henderson answered the questions about him by hitting home runs. And home runs win games, whether they are hit left-handed or right-handed.

Moreover, third baseman Mike Pagliarulo began perfecting that Yankee Stadium stroke, contributing more than the occasional home run. Ken Griffey and Ron Hassey helped. Left-handed hitting rookie Dan Pasqua, who hit a home run in his second major-league at-bat, and showed he might have a patented Yankee Stadium swing. The Yankees had their formula. It wasn't textbook Yankee Stadium but it was close enough to contend.

TRADITION

By winning all those pennants and championships, the New York Yankees created a tradition that inspired their players and intimidated their opponents. To be a Yankee demanded professionalism. Like the Montreal Canadiens in hockey, the Boston Celtics in basketball, or the Green Bay Packers in football, the Yankees became an inevitable force. When the championship game arrived, so did the Yankees.

Even the uniform became special. Over the years, many New York players remarked about the "pinstripe effect" that took place when they dressed. Wearing the pinstripes, players performed better, worked harder, and delivered more.

Some people felt the concept signified class. But this is not the correct word. The Yankees were wealthy, the management made sure they had the best players year after year, and they liked it that way.

The Yankees reinforced this competitive edge with attention to tradition. After all, they once had Babe Ruth, and they reminded themselves and everyone else of the fact by retiring his uniform number 3. Likewise, they retired, among others, Lou Gehrig's 4, Casey Stengel's 37, Mickey Mantle's 7, and Yogi Berra and Bill Dickey's 8. They placed monuments to their greats in center field, just as the Celtics placed

Known as "The House That Ruth Built," Yankee Stadium with its short right fence was a good friend to left-handed hitters like Mantle and Maris.

championship banners from the rafters of Boston Garden and the Canadien pictures of former greats in their locker room.

Furthermore, the Yankees played in a ballpark that was regal. It was nicknamed "The House That Ruth Built," a phrase that did its best to invoke the gods of baseball. The distinctive facade ornamenting the roof made the park look a bit like an opera house. It was baseball with a touch of art.

Conversely, any opponent wanting to overtake the Yankees had to confront this tradition. With the pennant at stake, you couldn't expect to just walk into Yankee Stadium and beat the Yankees. In a tight race, you confronted that famous Yankee logo. You had DiMaggio, Ruth, and Gehrig peeking over your shoulder.

Given such a situation, it is no surprise

Yankee legends honored in centerfield.

**Donning a pinstriped 24,
Rickey Henderson tops off the
1985 superstar line-up.**

New traditionalist Dave Winfield waits for a "fat" pitch.

Four of baseball's greats get together to talk over old times—Billy Martin, Stan Musial, Whitey Ford, and Mickey Mantle.

Don Baylor is an important element to the '85 Yankee formula.

Mattingly setting standards of his own.

that the Yankees win the close ones. In 1949, the Boston Red Sox came to Yankee Stadium for the final two games of the season. They needed only one victory to remain ahead of the Yankees for the pennant. They never got it. New York won the first game 5–4 to forge a tie entering the final game of the season. In the last game, Vic Raschi fired a five-hitter for a 5–3 victory. The Yankees were on their way to five straight World Series championships.

In 1978, the mystique worked for the Yankees and against the Boston Red Sox. Trailing first-place Boston by 14 games in July, the Yankees created a tie. Then they won the division in a one-game playoff with Bucky Dent hitting his historic three-run homer.

The mystique continued in the postseason. After losing the first two games of the World Series, they rebounded to win the next four games.

Again, the Yankees had found a way to win. They were seeking another in 1985.

3

A LONG WAY TO TRANQUILITY

The new manager began shaping the team by releasing reliever Dale Murray and adding a coach. Martin was aware that his presence would create tension, an ingredient, he feels, is necessary for a competitive edge. To soften that edge a bit, he hired retired Detroit Tiger slugger Willie Horton as "tranquility coach," a sort of diplomatic hatchet man. When he wanted to deliver a message without causing friction, Martin would pass the word through Horton. If he wanted to rouse a player, he would deal with the man personally. No one lights a fire better than Billy.

There certainly was no shortage of kindling. His starting pitching was inconsistent at best and his bullpen, overworked at a ridiculously early stage of the season, was exasperatingly ineffective. The defense was in shambles—making a string of 14 errors over a seven-game span in April—and his hitters were squandering opportunities. While Yogi could not bring himself to chew out players he believed weren't giving their best, Martin had no lack of initiative in that area.

But Texas was not cooperating. The 7–5 loss was followed by an 8–4 shelling the next evening. Phil Niekro gave up eight runs on 10 hits in six innings, and his record dropped to 3–2. The Yankees finished April having lost five straight, eight of their last nine. They were last in the AL East at 6–12, 5½ games behind Baltimore and Toronto.

On May 1, Martin began to gamble. He benched Winfield and Baylor, playing Omar Moreno in right and Hassey as designated hitter against knuckleballer Charlie Hough. Hassey went 4-for-4 with four RBI and Whitson finally got his first victory in a 5–1 decision, with help from Righetti, who worked the final four innings.

The team returned to New York on May 2, an off day, and the city had an extra day to think about Billy's maneuvers in the series finale at Texas. The team held a mandatory workout. The next day, Martin made his '85 Yankee Stadium debut against Kansas City and gave the Royals a dose of "Billy Ball," the term coined to describe Martin's tendency to scratch for

The long, middle part of the season had its ups and downs for the Yanks. Here, Baylor states his case to the ump.

runs with speed, cunning, and opportunism. The Bombers scored a season-high seven runs, created in part by two stolen bases and a pair of hit-and-run singles. The outburst made it a little easier to overlook the triple play the Royals pulled off on a Henderson line drive. Only a little over 20,000 fans turned out, possibly a protest over the firing of Yogi Berra. Martin was unfazed.

"They'll come out," he said. "We'll start winning. People won't come out when you're losing, but they forget everything when you win."

The Yankees completed a three-game sweep of the Royals. Guidry notched his first complete game, a four-hit shutout, and Baylor went 3-for-3 with a homer and four RBI. The next day Niekro and Righetti combined on a 6–2 victory powered by four homers. Ken Griffey got his first at-bat of the series when Kansas City finally went to a right-hander in relief and promptly cracked his first homer of the

Martin needed to stir things up, so he put Ron Hassey in as DH. Ron obliged with a round-tripper.

year. After the game he repeated a demand he had made in 1984, asking King to trade him.

DOME DOLDRUMS

Before flying to Minnesota, Martin placated Don Baylor by announcing he would no longer platoon the designated hitter. For about five days things were going smoothly. But in Minnesota, Martin broke this spate of tranquility. The Twins took a 7–3 lead thanks to three fly balls apparently lost by Yankees against the milky backdrop of the ceiling at the Metrodome. Whitson fell to 1–4, lasting just 1⅔ innings

The Twins look like a clean-cut, straight-forward ball club, but they have a ballpark in Minnesota that gives their opponents fits.

Don Baylor hustles back to first.

The Twins caused the Yanks all sorts of trouble in the Metrodome, but back in the Bronx the tide changed. Dale Berra takes a gunshot from Dave Winfield to tag the overzealous Greg Gagne out at third. Below, Mickey Hatcher makes it safely to third.

and giving up nine hits. After the game, Martin was livid.

"This ballpark should be banned from baseball," he barked. "If you win or lose a ball game on fly balls like that it doesn't matter. But you have major-league ballplayers coming in here and made to look like Little Leaguers. They paid 40 million dollars to [former Twin owner] Calvin Griffith for this ball club. You'd think the new owner here could spend some money on some blue paint for the damn ceiling. Tell them they don't put pockets in coffins. We come in here playing good baseball and we're made to look like a circus team. It's a Little League ballpark. And when they play the All-Star Game here, the whole world is going to see what kind of place this is."

After the game, the Yankees filed a formal protest with the American League

over conditions in the stadium. The protest eventually was denied.

On May 8, the Twins took an 8–6 victory, and Joe Cowley was knocked out after giving up five runs in the first and a two-run homer to Kent Hrbek in the fourth for a 7–3 lead. Martin was so disgusted with his starter he sent pitching coach Mark Connor to yank him. He later announced Montefusco would take Cowley's place in the rotation.

"He [Cowley] didn't keep us in the game," Martin groused. "We're down five runs right off the bat. One pitch, four runs, one pitch, two runs. Plus, you can't catch a walk. The guy walked four batters. He's got to show me more than that."

The Twins kept a hot streak going with the two-game sweep of the Yankees, marking their 10th straight 10-hit game. After the second game, Minnesota Twin manager Billy Gardner had some fun at New York's expense.

"I suppose George is now going to have to hire a dome coach to go with his tranquility coach and administrative coach," he said. "When we get to New York next week I'm going to protest too, because my ball players are liable to lose fly balls in the Big Dipper. They could get confused by shooting stars."

When the Twins got to Yankee Stadium, they paid for their laughs.

GATOR AID

One of the first portents of a good Yankee season came from the pitching mound in early May in Kansas City. It was there that New York took two of three games from the Royals. On May 10, Baylor's two-run homer in the eighth helped Ron Guidry to a 6–4 victory. This started Guidry on a streak that would draw comparisons to his 1978 Cy Young season. Being able to count on Guidry didn't make the division title a foregone conclusion, but it was one of the necessities.

In 1978, Guidry, born in Cajun Country,

truly was "Louisiana Lightning." His fastball came in consistently at 93 miles per hour or better, exploding past batters who batted a collective .193 against him. His slider was simply the most unhittable pitch in baseball.

"I used to just throw the ball past people," he said. "That was no fun."

His teammates always seemed to get a kick out of it, though. He won his first 13 decisions that season on his way to a 25–3 record for a major league record .893 winning percentage. His nine shutouts tied Babe Ruth's American League record for most by a left-hander, set in 1916. Eight times he struck out 10 or more batters, including a club-record 16 against the Angels. He finished with a 1.75 ERA, the lowest since 1966 when Sandy Koufax posted a 1.73.

The Yankees won 30 of the 35 games Guidry started that year, and in the five losses scored a total of only seven runs. He was a stopper in the truest sense of the word. Fifteen of his victories followed Yankee losses. When it came time to vote for the Cy Young Award, he was the unanimous choice, the first in the league since Denny McLain in his 31-victory season for the Tigers in 1968.

ADJUSTMENTS

In 1985, though, Guidry was using finesse. Compared with former years, his fastball was good, but only fast—around 90 mph. Guidry, nicknamed "Gator," had to make some adjustments. Nothing radical, just subtle changes. Fine-tuning. He started to "cut" his fastball, turning it over ever so slightly, almost like a screwball. It started running away from right-handed hitters, almost a reverse slider. By adding a little cunning to his repertoire, like an occasional straight change-up, the Gator became as dangerous as ever. He would win 12 straight decisions before Texas finally caught on to him July 26.

"You don't just wake up one morning

In 1985, the Gator's fastball had slowed some since this performance in the World Series.

Ron Guidry "relearned" pitching and put together 11 straight wins this year.

Yankee ace Marty Bystrom makes a comeback after an elbow injury.

George "The Boss" Steinbrenner juggles success and tradition.

The Dynamic Duo.

and decide you're going to be a different kind of pitcher," he insisted. "I'm still a power pitcher. But now I give hitters something else to think about. They can't go up to the plate just looking for two pitches. They have to respect the other stuff. But I don't throw junk.

"The confidence is still the same. When I went to pitch in '78, I didn't think I'd get beat. I didn't think the team would get beat. Sometimes I feel like that now."

On May 11, the Yankees made it two straight over the Royals with an 11–4 whipping. Baylor hit a grand slam in the nine-run fourth, the team's biggest inning in five years.

Fisher picked up the save for starter Rasmussen with two innings of no-hit, three-strikeout ball. With the chance to make it 11 straight victories over Kansas City, New York stumbled in the series wrap-up. Righetti made a throwing error on a potential inning-ending double play with the score tied in the ninth, and Jim Sundberg bounced a double over the wall to pull out a 6–5 Royal victory.

The Yankees hit into three crucial double plays, one by Winfield after an intentional walk to Mattingly that loaded the bases. The big man was 0-for-5 in the game, failing to advance six runners, three in scoring position. His batting average was down to .245 and he was 5-for-32 with men in scoring position.

"You've got to figure he's going to come out of it soon," Martin said.

Winfield promised he would and the team would be that much better off once he broke out. In the last nine games, Henderson had gone 18-for-44, raising his average to .286, foreshadowing what was to come in June.

In May, it was disclosed that Steinbrenner had hired former FBI agents to tail his ball players in certain cities. It was not a new tactic; owners have often put private detectives on such cases. Then came some amusing headlines: Don Mattingly and Dale Berra were arrested for urinating in public in Kansas City. Then as the team tore through a six-game winning

streak, Steinbrenner went public with his reasons for firing Yogi.

"What it comes down to, is that I'm entitled to change my mind," he said. "I felt I had to make a change, and if everybody in business operated on a policy of never changing their minds, there would be a lot more bankrupt companies than there are today.

"Last year I made a firm commitment to Yogi, and I stayed with him the whole year despite the fact we were 14 games out. Sure we played the best baseball of anyone in the second half, but we were never a threat. I pleaded with Yogi this year to be ready to get off to a fast start because everybody in the division was stronger. He promised me that he would and I shouldn't worry."

THERE IS UNITY HERE—BAYLOR

Baylor decided it was time to state the case for the players.

"There is unity on this team," he said. "There is great unity. I really believe we're going to play through all this stuff. We're going to play through FBI guys following us around, and we're going to play through mandatory workouts. We're here to play baseball, even with the things that go on here. This team is not without discipline. We were just playing bad. We had some guys get off to slow starts at the plate, but now those guys—me, Griffey, Mattingly—are starting to hit. It's no more complicated than that."

Yankee pitching started to come around near the All-Star break, and the coaches began to look to the minor leagues for future talent. Here pitching coach Mark Connor gives a few hints to first round draft pick Rick Balabon.

Dave is all smiles after his triple to centerfield scored two runs against Boston.

Although Henderson had a slow start at the plate, once on base he stole opponents' confidence.

Baylor's grand slam homer was a sight for sore eyes.

Hit the deck! Willie Randolph is brushed aside from an inside pitch.

There was no turning point to this Yankee season. Much of it hinged on how Martin would mesh with his club and how willing the players would be to let it happen. It started by degrees. This statement by Baylor, though somewhat grudging, was the first sign things would work out.

Back at the stadium, the Yankees illustrated Baylor's point. The Twins jumped to an 8–0 lead, knocking out Whitson in the second. The crowd of just 15,136 chanted "Let's Go Mets." A five-run fifth put New York back in the game and Mattingly tagged Ron Davis for a three-run homer in the bottom of the ninth to give the Yanks a 9–8 victory. Henderson was hit in the elbow with a fastball by Mike Smithson and did not bat the next five games. The next day, Montefusco gave up five runs in the first four innings but Griffey drilled a grand slam in the seventh to lift the Yankees to a 10–7 victory. In his last eight games, Griffey was hitting .429 with three homers and 11 RBI.

Against the Rangers on May 15, the Yankees blew a four-run lead. Griffey made a leaping catch and threw out Curtis Wilkerson at the plate, and Randolph flagged down a potential game-winning line drive in the ninth to hold the tie. In the 10th, Winfield's aggressive base running pulled out a 6–5 victory. Winfield led off with a walk, stole second, and took third after a flyout to left center with a headfirst slide, beating a good throw from Gary Ward. On a slow roller to first, Winfield broke for the plate and Pete O'Brien bobbled the ball trying to hurry his throw home.

"Let's put it this way," Winfield said. "If they would have gotten me, the catcher would have had a headache tomorrow. It's different every day around here. Everyone contributes. It's a long season, but I think we've hit our low point, already."

Then, Righetti suffered a broken toe,

Yankee third baseman Andre Robertson robs Hal McRae of a hit.

Bobby Meacham is taken out at third by Brewer Charlie Moore.

Unity, Fraternity, Pinstripes Forever!

stubbing it against a doorjam. It sidelined him for seven games. Against the Angels, Martin used Guidry in relief of Niekro, and Don Cooper finished a three-hit, 6–0 blanking. A 6–1 victory by Cowley and Fisher the following day gave the Yankees six straight.

"This is baseball at its very best," Martin said. "The timely hits, the suicide squeeze. And when Winfield gets going, we're going to be awesome."

Even with Winfield slumping at the plate, getting just three hits in his last 21 at-bats with two RBI, Billy liked the way he was playing.

"Take him out of the lineup?" Martin scoffed. "No way. The only way I'll sit him down is if he comes to me and tells me he's tired. I don't care if he's not hitting. He's a threat just standing at the plate, and he can do so many other things to beat you. He doesn't pout. He doesn't complain. He gives his all. He's the kind of guy managers love to have play for them. He's a fine individual."

Then Martin handed Winfield, hitting .244 with three home runs and 14 RBI on the season, the biggest compliment he could muster.

"He's a lot like Joe D. the way he can beat you on the bases or in the field, even when he's not hitting."

After a 6–10 start under Berra, the team was now 12–5 under Martin. New York scored 103 runs in Billy's first 16 games, compared with 57 in Yogi's 16, and committed six errors against 21.

"We knew we had a good team no matter who was managing," Guidry said. "We just didn't get a chance to prove that under Yogi. For him, we didn't hit, and we didn't play defense. You didn't expect this team not to hit. Billy's been doing a lot of things. Making other managers think more. Making a lot of little things happen and we're getting some breaks now. Under Yogi, we didn't get any breaks. You don't feel like you have to do it all alone. Somebody always seems to pick up for you when you're winning."

4

A TOUGH TOWN, NEW YORK

The crowing was a bit premature. After the six-game streak, the Yankees lost three of their next four games, dropping the last game of the Angel series 4–1. Whitson fell to 1–5 despite his best outing of the season to that point. The right-hander allowed two runs on six hits over six innings, but he gave up a homer to Brian Downing. The Yankees hit into three double plays, had two runners thrown out attempting to steal second in the same inning, and failed to score in the third when Winfield and Baylor did not hit the ball out of the infield with runners at first and second and one out.

The pressure was beginning to reach Whitson. His 14–8 record with the Padres was only his second winning season in the majors, where he was 35–43 lifetime. Perhaps even he couldn't understand why the Yankees signed him to a $4.4 million, five-year deal. On the road, he remained apart from his teammates, looking nervous and depressed. Pitching coach Mark Connor knew how Whitson felt.

"He's been through a terrible time," he said. "The thing with Ed is, he's just a country boy from Tennessee. All his career, he's pitched in Pittsburgh, San Francisco, Cleveland, and San Diego, laid back situations, all of them. Now he comes to New York with all that publicity, the big contract, and in his mind he has to be Sandy Koufax or Bob Gibson, a 25-game winner. But the fact is, he's never been that. He's just Ed Whitson and that's all we want him to be."

Whitson's eyes welled when he tried to explain his predicament: "It's been a terrible ordeal that I can't even bring myself to talk about," he said, "except to say I know the fans of New York are different from any others. Sometimes they don't see everything in a man's performance. If I was getting really belted, that's one thing. I don't think I'll ever be able to bring my family to the ballpark again."

As the losses piled up, so did the criticism. The derision from the fans grew worse with each unsuccessful outing. The walk back to the dugout after Martin signaled the bullpen became a gauntlet of

Steinbrenner signed Ed Whitson to a multi-million dollar contract. With a 1–5 start, Steinbrenner, the fans, and most importantly Whitson were discouraged.

verbal abuse. After one loss, he was accosted by a carfull of irate fans and had to run a red light to escape harassment. For Whitson, New York was the toughest of towns and he wasn't mastering it.

FIGHTING FOR .500

The Yankees moved on to Seattle, to play in their old nemesis, the Kingdome. If there was any hex on them in that building, it wasn't evident May 21. With Henderson back in the lineup, they pounded out 15 hits. Henderson belted a three-run homer and Winfield went 4 for 6. Guidry left after eight innings, having allowed three hits, and Cooper mopped up. Moreno, relegated to the bench, asked to be traded, but there were no takers for his big salary. In mid-August, Steinbrenner would release him despite having to pay two more seasons left on a $750,000-per-year deal.

The next night, the bats were quieted by Matt Young. The lefty threw a three-hitter, striking out 10 and retiring the last 16 Yankees for a 4–1 victory. A difficult act to follow, but Ken Phelps made a good run at it. Rumors of the Yankees trying to acquire a left-handed designated hitter never completely died. And it was even believed Phelps was being scouted first-hand in the series. He showed the Yankees what they were looking for, all right, clubbing a grand slam off Niekro to power Seattle to a 6–4 victory.

The Yankees left for Oakland, and the return of Rickey Henderson and Billy Martin to their old haunt, the Coliseum. Henderson was booed in every plate appearance, and was held hitless. Winfield picked matters up with a homer in the six-run fourth inning. Henderson gave a glimpse of what they were missing in the seventh. He reached on an error, stole second, went to third on a throwing error, and scored the final run in the 10–3 victory on a wild pitch. Cowley won his second straight since returning to the starting rotation, improving to 3–2.

Whitson pitched 9⅓ innings and gave up one run against the Royals, only to lose the game in extra innings.

May 25 was one of several low points for Righetti. After the Yankees scored a run to break a tie in the ninth, he walked in the winning run with two out in the bottom of the inning to suffer an 8–7 defeat. New York took out its frustration the next day, pounding out a 13–1 victory. Guidry was supported by a 19-hit attack: Henderson, 3 for 4; Sample, 4 for 5; Meacham, 4 for 4 with three RBI. The next day Rasmussen pitched a 1–1 tie into the ninth, but Righetti surrendered a leadoff homer to Dwayne Murphy in the 10th for a 2–1 loss, his fourth defeat of the year.

May 28, one game above .500 at 21–20, the Yankees returned to New York in fourth place. They were seven games behind the Blue Jays.

Home was the place to be for the Yankees. They took four straight from the Angels and Mariners at Yankee Stadium. In the opener against California, youth combined with experience in a 7–2 victory. Pagliarulo propelled Niekro to a 6–3 record with a three-run homer, his second of the year. The next night, Dan Pasqua, in his first major-league game, belted a shot into the right-field seats in his second at-bat and Mattingly drove in the winner for Cowley in a 3–1 triumph.

Against Seattle, Whitson was knocked out after four innings, but Fisher shut out the Mariners the rest of the way, and homers from Winfield, Baylor, and Andre Robertson sparked the victory. June 2 was Bat Day at the stadium, when Seattle dealt Rasmussen his third loss. Mattingly homered in the eighth. Niekro, 7–3, put the

A frequent scene in the beginning of the season

was Yankee ace Dave Righetti, coming on in relief.

Yankees back in the win column the next day, with 4-for-4, two-RBI support from Winfield in a 5–2 victory.

Again, New York could not sustain momentum, dropping their next three. Rookie Tim Birtsas and Jay Howell, who went to the A's in the Henderson trade, combined with Keith Atherton on a six-hit shutout. Cowley developed back spasms in the fifth and wound up with the 2–0 loss.

At Milwaukee, the Brewers shelled Whitson in a 6–1 decision. June 7, the Yankees wasted four homers, two by Winfield, and two late rallies, losing in the ninth, 10–9. Righetti squandered a lead in the eighth, and Charlie Moore's infield single with one out in the 10th pinned him with another loss. Guidry had his worst start of the year to that point, giving up six runs on 10 hits.

The next night, the Yanks edged the Brewers 2–1 in 13 innings. Pasqua tied the score in the ninth with a sacrifice fly off Rollie Fingers and Berra won it in the 13th with an RBI single to right. A 9–4 defeat the following game, however, gave them five losses in seven games, and with his pitching staff chronically arm weary, Martin was worried as the team entered a three-game homestand against the Blue Jays.

THE OLD MAN

He is called "Father Time." Just when you think his clock is winding down, Phil Niekro springs forward with another startling performance.

The 46-year-old master of the knuckleball is an enigma. Most former players his age are selling insurance or are behind a microphone. But "Knucksie," as he is known to his teammates, just keeps sending batters back to the dugout, shaking their heads after a few futile swats at the flutterball.

Niekro was considered washed up years ago. But he has defied the odds and in the process has become one of the all-time strikeout leaders. He entered the 1985 sea-son just 16 wins from 300 victories. Many times this year he took the mound against pitchers half his age.

The Ancient One came to the Yankees in 1984 after 10 years with the Braves. Atlanta manager Joe Torre felt Niekro was finished so he suggested the Braves not re-sign him. Yankee general manager Clyde King convinced Steinbrenner to sign Niekro to a two-year contract. It turned out to be a sound move.

Niekro was the club's winningest pitcher in 1984, getting off to a 4–0 start en route to a 16–8 record. He went into the All-Star break at 11–4 with a 1.84 ERA but tailed off in the second half. Some speculated his poor second half was a sign that either AL hitters had learned to time his knuckleball or he was finally on his way out. But the gray-haired right-hander confounded batters again in 1985. Niekro was strong the first 2½ months of the season, winning seven of his first 10 decisions. Although he faltered in midseason, when the Yankees got hot in August, the old man showed that his pilot light wasn't extinguished yet.

BOB WHO?

Buried in the bullpen was Bob Shirley, who had pitched just 5⅔ innings since Yogi's departure. At one point, Shirley had gone 21 games without an appearance. His teammates had started a lottery revolving around his next appearance. When Martin gave him a start against Toronto, the Yanks hit the jackpot.

Shirley worked 6⅓ innings, allowing one run on six hits, and earned a 4–2 victory, his first of the season. Winfield injured his left knee in a late-inning rundown, however, and missed the next game, which proved to be Whitson's biggest heartbreak of all. He went 9⅓ innings, allowed one run on six hits while striking out seven. His good fortune even reached the point where the stadium fans finally got behind him, chanting "Ed-die, Ed-die." Berra tied the score in the bottom of the ninth. In the

At 46, Phil Niekro is still an important cog in the Yankee pitching machine. His knuckleball gives both opposing hitters and Yankee catchers more than they can handle.

In an important series against the Seattle Mariners, Dale Berra takes no chances at being tagged out as he sends pitcher Brian Snyder sprawling to the ground.

Yankee pitching got off to a rocky start this year. With nowhere else to go, Martin went to the bullpen and pulled Bob Shirley to start. Billy had no regrets as Shirley worked 6⅓ innings against the Blue Jays, giving up only three hits.

11th, however, Willie Randolph committed an error that led to a three-run rally and Fisher was tagged with the 4–1 defeat.

The next night's loss was just as disheartening. Guidry left with a 2–1 lead after 7⅓, but Righetti and Bordi could not hold the lead. One out away from a save, Rags walked Jeff Burroughs on a 3–2 pitch, then surrendered an RBI double to Willie Upshaw. In the 10th, Bordi served

Timely hitting was the key to the Yanks' success during midseason. Gene Michael, third base coach, is happy to congratulate Mike on a round-tripper.

Mike Pagliarulo hits the deck to slip by the Angels catcher. Mike's 3-run home run was the game-winning hit that allowed the Bombers to beat the Angels in a crucial series.

up a homer to Rance Mulliniks, and the Blue Jays left town with a nine-game lead.

"In all my years, I don't think I've ever managed any better," Martin said on an off day before the Tigers came to town.

Then he launched into a monologue

Seattle Mariner captain Chuck Cottier is furious after being ejected from the game. As you can see, he takes base-stealing a bit too far.

about spring training.

"Now, I'm not knocking Yogi, but we need to work on a lot of little things—pickoffs, rundowns, cutoffs. The other day I asked the guys if they worked with the infield drawn in, and they said no, we didn't go over that. Then what the hell did they do in spring training?"

As if the Yankees couldn't get in enough trouble just playing games, off days be-came opportunities to air gripes in the press. Clyde King said Martin should use Shirley every four days. Martin responded bitterly. "Gutsy," Martin said, quoting King's description of Shirley's perfor-mance against the Blue Jays. "I'm not sur-prised. I've seen him do it before," Billy mimicked the general manager. "Where did he see him do it? Hasbrouck Heights? Secaucus? Shirley didn't pitch that much for Yogi, either, did he?"

Mattingly was asked what he thought about the mandatory off-day workouts. He said he didn't like them and neither did Billy. Steinbrenner responded angrily to Mattingly.

"If he's upset at working out, that's too damn bad," the owner fumed. "He ought to talk to the cab drivers or steelworkers about working hard. Or talk to the farmers around his Indiana home who are losing their farms. I'm fed up with his attitude. Last year I thought he was a fine, All-American type boy. With that incident in Kansas City and his attitude now, I'm not so sure. Mattingly ought to realize that his lack of hitting is killing us."

At that time, Mattingly was hitting .288, 55 points off his league-leading pace in 1984.

5

TURNING TO HENDERSON

The Yankees were home against Detroit for a three-game weekend set, the first time New York faced the World Series champs all season. They were helpless in the opener as Walt Terrell and Willie Hernandez combined on a five-hitter. Tom Brookens, Barbaro Garbey, Kirk Gibson, and Larry Herndon supplied solo homers in consecutive innings in the 4–0 victory. New York lost 10–8 the next day after being down early. Shirley checked the Tigers 2–1 in the finale Sunday.

New York moved to Baltimore and swept a three-game series, which marked the beginning of Henderson's assault on American League pitchers. The Yankee bats turned hot. New York outscored the Orioles 26–4. Henderson went 10 for 3 in the three games with five stolen bases.

The one setback New York suffered in Baltimore was the loss of catcher Butch Wynegar, who was struck in the head by a foul ball while on-deck. Wynegar was looked upon by some as the one indispensable Yankee starter. But Ron Hassey did an outstanding job in Wynegar's absence.

In the third game of the set, he cracked two homers.

SUMMER HEAT

The Yankees were waiting for Henderson to finally break loose and the time came in the middle of June. After getting off to a slow start because of his early-season ankle injury, he provided his own summer heat. Despite New York losing three of four to the Tigers in Detroit, Henderson continued the pace he started in Baltimore, ripping three more homers and swiping four bases.

The Orioles came into New York for three games and again the Yankees swept the Birds, with Henderson stealing six bases to run his total to 36. During this burst, Henderson raised his average to well over .350 and his startling performance convinced fans to vote him to the All-Star team.

When Henderson came to New York from Oakland in a seven-player deal during last December's winter meetings, Stein-

Henderson sidesteps Tiger first baseman Darrel Evans as a pickoff throw goes wild—he took second and later scored the winning run on a hit by Dave Winfield.

Billy and Earl happily greet one another before the game, but Earl realizes that with Billy back in charge the Yanks will be a threat.

brenner felt he had added the final piece to what potentially could be the most powerful lineup in the American League.

The 26-year-old outfielder is one of baseball's jewels. He brought a career .291 average into this season. He covers the expansive outfield in Yankee Stadium as well as anyone. And his power is not to be underestimated. He may be the quintessential leadoff hitter who steals bases but by no means should he be classified a singles hitter.

Last year, the A's asked Henderson to hit more for power and he responded with a career-high 16 homers. By August 5 of this season, he had surpassed that total.

Oriole second baseman Rich Dauer seems to be getting some advice, as Rickey concludes his second steal of the evening.

Take a good look at Henderson and it's clear where his strength comes from. He is 5'10" and 195 pounds, a former high school football player. He has powerful thighs and muscular forearms and biceps. Since he is basically a line-drive, pull hitter, he has no trouble reaching the left-field fence at Yankee Stadium. What makes Henderson so tough at the plate is his deep crouch, which, says Oriole manager Earl Weaver, makes it almost impossible to get him out. Henderson reduces the strike zone and draws his walks. And once he is on first, the pitcher and catcher might just as well concede second.

With Henderson hot, New York surged. By the All-Star break, the Yankees had cut Toronto's lead to 2½ games.

BLUE JAY HUNTING

On July 1, New York visited Toronto and won two of three. The Yanks were denied a sweep when the Blue Jays took the finale 3–2 in 10 innings. But following that loss, the Yankees returned home to play three teams from the West, against whom they rarely lose.

On July 4, Guidry tossed a six-hit complete game to lead the Yanks to a 3–2 victory over the Twins, running his record to 10–3. After winning again Friday, the Yanks played a doubleheader Sunday, following a Saturday rainout. With the score 2–2 in the 11th inning of the first game, Winfield led off with his 10th homer, off of Twin reliever Curt Wardle, to win it. In the

**A rare strikeout for Rickey—Walt Terrell was hot
against the Yankees in this June 14th outing.**

Toronto manager and former Yankee coach Bobby Cox greets Billy Martin before a game.

second game, the Yankees were steaming. Griffey led a four-homer attack with two homers and six RBI as New York ran the Twins out of town with a 14–2 triumph to cap a four-game sweep.

The Yanks then took two of three from the Royals and battered the Rangers in four straight games to go into the All-Star break at 49–36.

STRIKE

Following the All-Star game, the Yankees returned to that pleasure dome in Minnesota for a four-game set. Reacting to Martin's early season complaints of the circus-like atmosphere at the Metrodome, the Twin management had the dome's ceiling repainted.

No matter. New York dropped the first game of the series. The Yankees rebounded to win the next three with Guidry

Blue Jay Len Matusek slides safely into third in front of Dale Berra during Toronto's 11th inning rally that beat the Yankees 4–1.

Ricky is on his way to robbing a hitter of a sure homer.

Rickey is caught off-guard as Royal Steve Balboni puts on the tag.

The Orioles run down Rickey between second and third.

Picked off—courtesy of Juan Agosto and Greg Walker of the White Sox.

Bill Buckner is the victim of this Henderson theft.

Henderson scores while Marc Hill waits for the throw.

The beginning of a ruckus: Henderson was called safe, then out, for a double play.

Bobby Meacham tries to prevent Blue Jay Tony Fernandez from completing a double play.

and Niekro winning back-to-back complete games to end the series. While the Yanks were taking three of four from the Twins, the Blue Jays were splitting four games with Oakland. On July 21, New York was within 1½ games of first.

But not so fast. The Yankees lost three straight to the Royals, whom New York had beaten in seven of the nine previous games. Things got worse as the Yanks dropped two of three at Texas. They closed this woeful roadtrip by losing three straight to Cleveland after having won the first two games of the series.

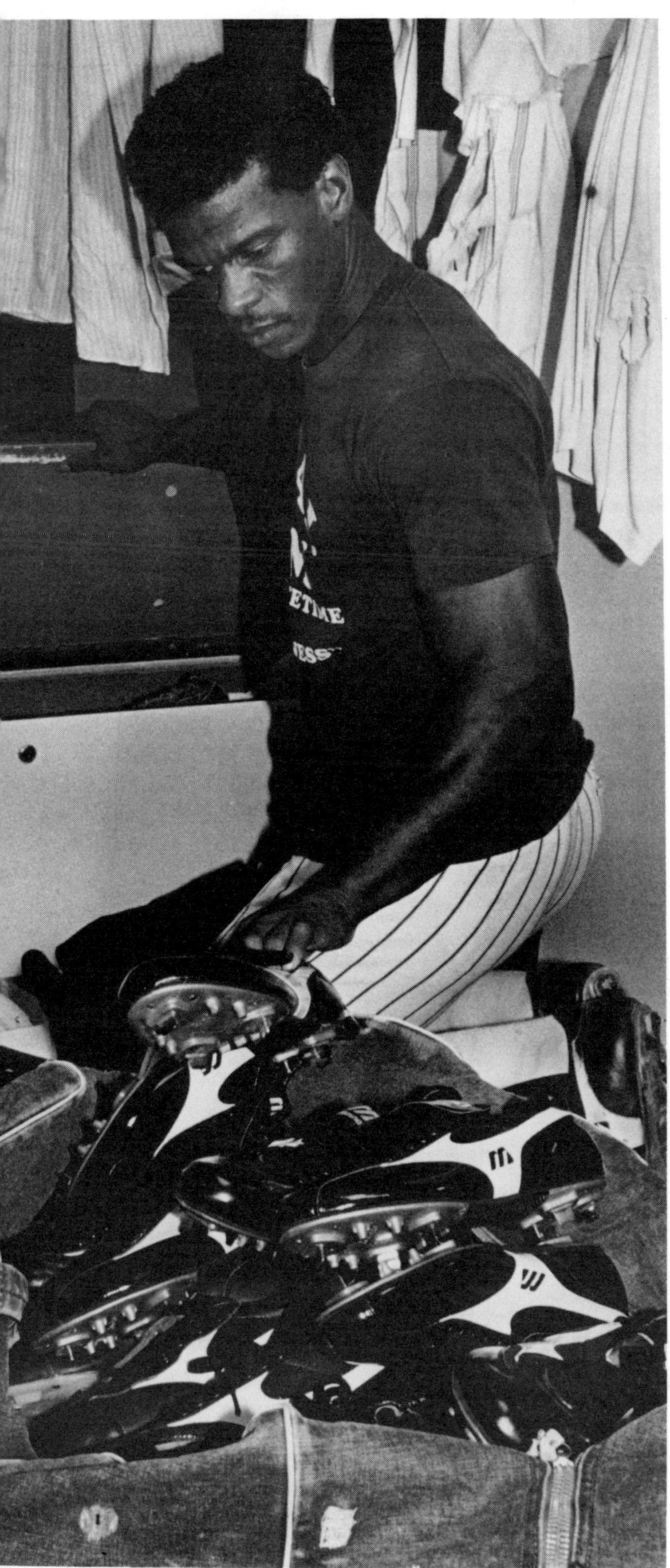

Henderson unhappily empties his locker—the strike was on.

The Yankees went 6–9 on that trip while the Blue Jays went 12–3 to open an 8½-game lead over New York by August 1. Going home did not cure the Yankees' problems. They split four games with the White Sox. One of the losses came against Tom Seaver, who chalked up his 300th career victory August 4 before a capacity crowd. Guidry beat Chicago the next night to raise his record to 14–4.

Then major-league baseball stopped. A strike was called August 6 by the players with the Yankees nine games back. A prolonged walkout like the 50-day strike in 1981 would virtually end the season. But the dispute was settled in two days and by August 8, the players were back on the field.

The Yankees were home for a doubleheader against the Indians. Marty Bystrom, making a comeback from offseason elbow surgery, started the opener and went five innings. Winfield cracked homers in his first two at-bats to send the Yanks to an 8–1 victory. The Yankees used the longball again to take the nightcap 7–6 as Mattingly belted two homers and Baylor connected for his 19th.

On a roll, the Yankees invaded Fenway Park in Boston and swept the Red Sox in a weekend series to move within seven games of the Jays. The Yankees traveled to Chicago and beat the White Sox in the opener of their three-game set to extend their winning streak to six. The White Sox took the next game but New York concluded the series with a victory—the first of seven straight.

The Yankees returned to New York for a three-game homestand against the Red Sox. They repaid Boston for those five embarrassing early season losses by completing a three-game sweep to move within five games of Toronto on August 18. New York took off for an eight-game West Coast swing. Toronto's lead was eroding, as the Yankees won six of seven from

California and Seattle to trail by three games on August 25.

A MIRACLE CATCH

Ken Griffey's performance typified just how well the Yankees were playing in August. He had never been happy in New York, but as the pennant race intensified, Martin took comfort in having his bat from the left side and his spectacular glove in the outfield.

A member of the Cincinnati Red championship teams in 1975 and 1976, Griffey was obtained by the Yankees in 1981 and signed to a six-year contract worth over $1 million a year. With the signing came a promise he would play regularly. That was not to be the case.

Uncertain about his knees—battered after years of playing on artificial turf—the Yankees switched Griffey to first base where he was inconsistent. As a result, his playing time was curtailed. Several times Griffey asked to be traded, for he was accustomed to playing every day. Since joining the Yanks, Griffey had not played more than 127 games in a season.

When he did play, though, he produced. While he did not have the ability to carry the team like Winfield or Mattingly, he could hurt opponents with his bat or his glove. At 35, he no longer had the thoroughbred speed, but there was still life in the legs.

Griffey spent nine years with the Reds. He was a clutch player in the batter's box and in the outfield.

This year he made catches that bordered on miraculous. In the Yankee home-opening series, he robbed Ron Kittle of a homer in the ninth inning by leaping over the left-field fence to preserve a 4–4 tie. Don Baylor then won it with a homer in the ninth. The next game Griffey made a catch reminiscent of Sandy Amoros's heart-stopper against Yogi Berra in the 1955 World Se-

Ken Griffey gives it his all.

Griffey lunges for a pop fly.

Griffey races down Carlton Fisk's long fly, which he caught, then doubled up Ron Kittle.

Safe! Henderson beats out Twins catcher Dave Engel.

ries. Griffey went far into the left-field corner to make an outstretched catch of a shot by Carlton Fisk. That catch enabled the Yankees to double Kittle off first and kill a White Sox rally.

But those were mere preludes to the opus of August 19 against Boston. At the time the Yankees badly needed a win to stay close to the Blue Jays. With the Yankees up 6–5 in the ninth, Marty Barrett of the Red Sox drove a pitch off Shirley deep to left. Griffey raced to the fence, planted his foot halfway up the 8-foot padded wall, and vaulted into the third row of seats. He snared the ball, then juggled it momentarily. He dropped to the ground, the ball secure—it was one of the greatest catches ever made in Yankee Stadium.

6
CLOUT
WINFIELD AND MATTINGLY

Dave Winfield is 6'6" and 220 pounds. He cuts a fierce figure for any pitcher to look at. Put a bat in his hands and watch out! Looked upon by many as the most complete player in the major leagues, Winfield can not only beat you with bruising power but with the simple base hit as well.

In 1981 he signed his ballyhooed contract with the Yankees. The next year he hit a career-high 37 homers with 106 RBI, all the more impressive considering he is a right-handed hitter playing half his games in Yankee Stadium. He followed with 32 homers and 116 RBI the next season.

Last year, with the Yankees out of the pennant race by June, Winfield concentrated on a career goal—winning a batting title. He and Mattingly went to the wire. Winfield lost out in the final game of the regular season. The final averages had Mattingly at .343 and Winfield at .340. It was the first time since 1977 teammates finished 1–2 in the batting race. Rod Carew and the late Lyman Bostock of the Twins were on top then, but were separated by 52 points.

This season Winfield started slowly because of spring training injuries. But by mid-August he surpassed 1984's homer total of 19 and was on his way to his fourth straight 100 RBI season. He was the leading vote-getter of all American League outfielders. It was his ninth All-Star appearance. At that point, the Yankees were 2½ games behind Toronto.

"I always enjoy playing [in the All-Star Game]," Winfield said. "But I'd rather be in first place. I'd rather be in front and have other teams try and catch us. That's where you get real joy and happiness."

HITTING STRIDE

Winfield is a multi-dimensional ball player. As a warning to anyone naïve enough to try and take an extra base on him, don't even think of it. You have no chance. The odds are better for scaling Mt. Everest.

Winfield, who pitched at the University of Minnesota, has such a deadly arm that runners have virtually given up challenging it.

The Yankees moved Winfield to right

Ouch! Winfield takes one in the back.

field in 1985 when they obtained Henderson. He alternated between left and center since joining the Yanks, but feels more comfortable in right, where he used to play for the San Diego Padres in 1973.

Winfield was drafted in three pro sports. He never spent a day in the minors and was an immediate success as a major leaguer. In his first full season in 1974 he ripped 20 homers. His home run total slipped the next two years but his overall run production and batting average got better. From 1977–79, he put together

Dave Winfield hangs tough by sliding safely into first.

three outstanding seasons. In '79, Winfield pounded out 34 homers, drove in 118 runs, and batted .308.

Winfield was eligible for free agency after the 1980 season. Realizing his market value, he asked for the moon and George Steinbrenner accommodated. He landed the biggest contract in baseball history— $23 million over 10 years.

Winfield may have reported to spring training in 1981 as the highest paid player, but he was still not top banana on that Yankee team. Still around was a man named Reginald Martinez Jackson—the self-proclaimed "straw that stirs the drink." And there was friction between the superstars.

MONEY PLAYERS

Winfield's lifelong dream was to play in the World Series. In his eight years in San Diego, the Padres never finished higher than fourth. In his first year with the Yan-

Winfield does his version of the rumba. Positions 1 and 2.

Rickey Henderson congratulates Winfield on his homerun.

Winfield dives back to first after Dan Pasqua flies out, but long-legged Bobby Grich is already on the bag.

kees, he was on a winner. After taking the first two games of the World Series against the Dodgers, the Yankees already had the champagne chilled, but the corks never popped. Los Angeles steamrolled New York in four straight games. It was the last time the Yankees would advance to the postseason.

Winfield was inconsequential in the World Series, going 1 for 22, his only hit coming in the final game, a meaningless

Indian pitcher Neal Heaton blows one by a swinging Winfield.

Winfield charges home.

single. Despite his outstanding regular season stats, Winfield came under fire—most notably by Steinbrenner—for not being the money player Jackson was. But the fact is that the Yankees have not been in any money games the last three years. Since 1982, there has been no pennant race for the Yankees. They finished fifth once and third twice.

But with the Yankees in a pennant race in 1985, and with money games to be played, the public—and Steinbrenner—have come to appreciate Winfield's full worth.

MAKING IT

When you look on the field and see Don Mattingly scooping grounders off the dirt or lining fastballs over the fence, you remember how close he came to not making it at all. It's not that Mattingly lacked talent or drive. It's just that he had only played in the minors and the Yankees preferred veterans.

The Rangers catch Mattingly in a rundown.

Mattingly doubles and slides safely into second as Julio Franco dives for the tag.

The Yankees liked to sign free agents and make trades. That often meant giving up minor-league talent in exchange. Sometimes the theory worked, sometimes it didn't. The Yankees let a lot of talent get away, and that talent is now all over the majors.

During home games, the Yankee scoreboard posts information on minor-league games. Mattingly's name showed up often. The fans knew about him. It was only a question of whether he would reach the Bronx. Mattingly was selected by the Yankees in the 19th round of the June 1979 free-agent draft and was signed by scouts Jax Robertson and Gust Poulos.

To many players, their first professional experience is difficult—playing away from home and competing against more talented players. Mattingly was not intimidated. In fact, he showed every sign of being born to hit.

He played 53 games for the Yankees' farm team in the New York–Penn League

Mattingly is called back after the ball barely goes foul.

in 1979, hitting .349 and driving in 31 runs in only 166 at-bats. In 1980, he started to win awards. He hit a league-leading .358 for Greensboro and was named the South Atlantic League's Most Valuable Player. It was then that his name first started appearing on the Yankee scoreboard.

In 1981, he hit .314 at Nashville and became the Yankee minor league Player of the Year. Promoted to Class AAA in 1982, Mattingly hit .315 in 130 games at Columbus.

By 1983, Mattingly was about ready for the majors. He won the top rookie award at spring training and went north with the club. He was returned to Columbus and recalled on June 20 when Bobby Murcer retired. Thus, Mattingly became a Yankee who did not get away. It was not a case of luck, but simply good player development. Whether they knew it or not, the Yankees had baseball's next superstar.

Mattingly hit his first major-league homer off Boston's John Tudor on June 24. The homer was significant for a few reasons. First, Tudor was a left-hander, an indication of Mattingly's ability to hit lefties. Second, it was hit in Fenway Park, a difficult home-run park for left-handed hitters. If Mattingly could hit them there, he could hit them anywhere.

The 1983 season had its curious moments for Mattingly. He hit in 24 of 25 games from July 13 to August 11. He played second base in the completion of the famous Pine Tar game and batted only once. If he had collected a hit, it would have retroactively given him a 25-game hitting streak. When the year was finished, Mattingly owned a .283 average. The Little Leaguer from Evansville, Indiana, had arrived.

BATTLING BATS

Few sights in baseball are as pretty as the blossoming of a young talent. Mattingly was such a sight in 1984—even though the Yankees had to find a place for him to play. Yogi Berra had trouble finding him a steady spot in the field. With over-

Mattingly remains almost fanatically dedicated to becoming the best possible hitter he can be.

Winfield tosses his bat in disgust after striking out against the White Sox.

Mattingly honors the late Pete Sheehy, Yankee clubhouse manager, by wearing a black armband.

Don Mattingly takes a mouthful while diving into third.

Mattingly gives the "high five" to Winfield.

Rickey Henderson and Dave Winfield—Yankee stars on their way to the All-Star Game.

Winfield loses his helmet while safely sliding
into second.

Mattingly forces White Sox Ozzie Guillen to perform some ballet to complete a double play.

crowding at first base and the outfield, Mattingly had to undeniably assert his batting credentials. Berra's hand was forced and Mattingly stayed at first.

Playing every day, Mattingly became the first Yankee to lead the league in hitting since Mickey Mantle in 1956. He posted the highest average by a left-handed batter since Lou Gehrig's .351 in 1937. He made the American League All-Star team, was the top road hitter in the league, led the AL with 207 hits and 44 doubles, and led league first basemen with a .996 fielding percentage.

Still, the Yankees weren't a winner. They owned the best record in baseball after the All-Star break but finished well behind the division-leading Tigers. To do better in 1985 they would need Mattingly again.

But there was a hitch. Mattingly required arthroscopic knee surgery before the season. And with the knee on the mend, he spent hours reading at poolside during spring training. Whatever he read must have been beneficial. In his first spring at-bat, he hit a home run. He continued to recuperate. He continued to hit. All was fine.

Mattingly lets the world know how he feels when forced out at second to end the 7th inning against the Brewers. The Brewers went on to win the game 7–5.

Dave takes a breather at third.

Mattingly holds Tribe opponent close at first base.

Take May 13, for example. The Yankees trailed Minnesota 8–0 and eventually won on Mattingly's three-run homer with two out in the ninth. By August 20, he owned 16 game-winners, among the tops in the league. His two-homer game in Anaheim helped the Yankees beat the Angels 8–5 and keep the heat on Toronto.

Mattingly remains almost fanatically dedicated to becoming the best possible hitter. Before every game he studiously works on his stroke. He talks hitting with batting instructor Lou Piniella. Anyone listening might think they were overhearing Da Vinci and Edison discussing inventions.

Of course, Mattingly wasn't doing all the hitting himself, and that was the beauty of it. There was Henderson and Winfield and Baylor, and the rest of the 1985 Yankees.

"I'm kind of enjoying it," Mattingly said. "I just want to have a good season and be consistent. Put the bat on the ball, put it in play, and drive in runs when I have to."

And so he did. And so they did. Suddenly, the spat with Steinbrenner meant nothing. The managerial switch meant nothing. Henderson, Mattingly, Guidry, and Griffey were playing at the top of their games. So were Pagliarulo, Niekro, Righetti, and Winfield. The Yankees had done what their history demanded: they had created a pennant race.

APPENDIX
NEW YORK YANKEES
1985 ROSTER

PRINCIPAL OWNER   George M. Steinbrenner III
GENERAL MANAGER   Clyde King
MANAGER   Billy Martin
COACHES   Mark Connor (56), Willie Horton (48), Stump
Merrill (42), Gene Michael (40), Lou Piniella
(14), Jeff Torborg (44)
TEAM PHYSICIAN   Dr. John J. Bonam
TRAINERS   Gene Monahan, Mark Letendre

PITCHERS

No.	Name
53	Allen, Neil
43	Bordi, Rich
50	Bystrom, Marty
41	Cowley, Joe
54	Fisher, Brian
49	Guidry, Ron
26	Montefusco, John
35	Niekro, Phil
45	Rasmussan, Dennis
19	Righetti, Dave
29	Shirley, Bob
38	Whitson, Ed

CATCHERS

No.	Name
52	Espino, Juan
12	Hassey, Ron
27	Wynegar, Butch

INFIELDERS

No.	Name
2	Berra, Dale
23	Mattingly, Don
20	Meacham, Bobby
6	Pagliarulo, Mike
30	Randolph, Willie
18	Robertson, Andre

OUTFIELDERS

No.	Name
25	Baylor, Don
33	Griffey, Ken
24	Henderson, Rickey
21	Pasqua, Don
11	Sample, Billy
31	Winfield, Dave